Balboa Press books may be ordered through booksellers or by contacting:

Balboa Press
A Division of Hay House
1663 Liberty Drive
Bloomington, IN 47403
www.balboapress.com
844-682-1282

ISBN: 978-1-4525-1424-6 (sc)
ISBN: 978-1-4525-1425-3 (e)

Library of Congress Control Number: 2014908305

Print information available on the last page.

Balboa Press rev. date: 12/21/2022

# On The Farm

Caring stories for young children

## RIITTA KORPINEN

# Robyn Red Breast

Once upon a time near the farm house, there lived a little Robyn Red Breast. The sun was setting and she was terribly busy because she hadn't finished building her nest. She had been working all day.

The farm dogs saw what she was doing and wanted to help. They came and shook themselves and rolled on the ground so Robyn could collect the hair that fell out. With their help she had almost finished her nest.

Robyn's next-door neighbor Lady Rosella was watching her. She had already finished her nest and had laid her eggs in the cozy bed and was settling down to sleep.

As the sun went down there was a strange quietness in the air. The leaves and the grass were still. Robyn and Rosella saw grey clouds approaching, slowly getting closer and closer. Then they could smell the smoke. They looked at each other both very worried.

Rosella called out, "FIRE! We must fly away as fast as we can! Oh, what should I do? I cannot leave my nest and eggs! "Robyn had just put the last bit of soft grass in her nest and was ready to lay her eggs. Where would she lay her eggs if she had to leave the nest?

The two mothers were very afraid and didn't know what to do. Just then a family of big grey kangaroos hurriedly hopped past them. Mother kangaroo saw the worried birds up in the tree and stopped.

"Are you coming? The fire is catching up to us and we need to hurry. You can put your nests in my empty pouch, but you need to be fast."

Both birds took their nests and carefully placed them in the mother kangaroos pouch. Then they followed father kangaroo to the river. They felt safer at the riverbank, but to be completely safe they had to cross the river.

"Can you swim?" called Rosella to mother kangaroo.

"I am not a very good swimmer but I will try."

"What about my eggs?" asked Rosella.

"And what about my nest?" asked Robyn.

"They can float on the water. You will just need to fly above them and keep an eye on them," mother kangaroo replied.

The flames were getting close to the riverbank now and the kangaroos had to go into the water and try to swim to the other side of the river. Rosella and Robyn flew overhead keeping a close eye on their nests.

Finally they made it! They were all exhausted as the river was very wide and they had to use all their strength to reach the other side.

Father kangaroo was now out of the water and the rest of his family followed. The nests were gently floating on top of the water by the riverbank. With the help of the water creatures, the birds and kangaroos were able to find new branches to place Robyn and Roselle's nests.

"Thank you water, for saving us. Thank you water, for letting us drink from you," they all said. And calmness had started to return to their lives.

The night had settled in, and the stars were shining up above. Father kangaroo had one last look at his family, and at Lady Rosella, and at little Robyn Red Breast up in their nests. Then he fell happily asleep.

# Sunny the Farm Dog

Once upon a time, near a farmhouse at the edge of the woods, there was a little pond. The pond was decorated all around by water lilies, and was home to a family of ducks.

Father duck and mother duck were busily showing their seven ducklings how to find food from the bottom of the pond. They were diving in and out of the water, again and again.They were so busy diving, that they didn't see Sunny, the farm dog, coming to have a drink from the pond. Sunny saw the ducks. How funny they looked with their feathers poking up out of the water. He always wanted to play with the ducks, but they never wanted to play with him.

The ducks were afraid of Sunny. He was so big and his paws were so heavy. But because they were diving, the ducks didn't see Sunny, and he was so happy when the ducks didn't fly away. He slowly moved closer to them.He was just about to reach one of the ducklings, when father duck saw him.

Quickly father duck got out of the water and called out to his family.
"Dive in!" He called.
Then he stood at the edge of the pond, close to the dog and said, "Come and catch me if you can! I am much bigger than my little ducklings."Sunny thought,

"Alright, I will catch you then." But as always, when Sunny got close to him, father duck flew away.

In the meantime mother duck and the little ones had gone far away to safety.
Sunny didn't understand why the ducks always flew away. He would love to play hide and seek with them, but they didn't seem to know how to play. Just then there came a whistle and Sunny ran back to the farmhouse.

It was time for him to go with the farmer to get some firewood from the forest. Oh how he loved to hop in the truck and go for a drive.

Into the woods they went. Soon the truck stopped and Sunny's work started. Oh how he loved to carry the sticks into a pile. That was the best job he could ever think of.

The sun started to set down behind the trees, painting the sky with beautiful colors.Sunny was watching the farmer, who was getting ready to go back to the farmhouse. Then he heard the call; "Sunny, hop in the truck. It's time to go back" . . . Now Sunny knew it was getting close to the time when he got his reward after a hard days work. And here it was; a piece of cheese. YUM YUM!

Then he went to his bed on the verandah and lay down to have a rest.
He had a last look at the pond where the ducks were getting ready to go to bed and thought, I will teach you my favorite game tomorrow. Goodnight.

# The Fox

Once upon a time, not so long ago, the sun was shining and the roses were looking happy. The old woman was spinning wool, next to her window, on the farm. She was very happy because her sheep had given her lots of wool to make into warm things for winter. She had been spinning so much wool that her hands were getting shiny from the oil.

Sunny, the farm dog was snoozing peacefully next to her feet, but not for very long.

Suddenly the chooks and the rooster started to make a lot of noise in the chook pen. The old woman looked up through her window. What did she see but a pointy nose and a bushy tail. A Fox !

The old woman threw down the wool and started to run towards the chook house, Sunny racing along in front of her. The old woman shouted at the fox," Go away and leave my chooks alone!"The fox managed to get hold of one of her white chickens, but Sunny chased after the fox and because Sunny was very fast, the fox had to drop the chicken in order to run away. Sunny ran after him.

In the meantime, the old woman took the white chicken that was lying on the ground and started to calm her down by patting her and talking softly to her. When the old woman looked for the other chooks and the rooster, she found them hiding in the corner of the pen. She also saw the hole under the fence, between the rocks. That must be the place, where the fox had squeezed through to get into the chook house. She would have to ask the farmer to fix it when he came home from the fields.

She took the white, frightened chicken into the shed and made her a cozy bed in the box with some straw. She gave her some water and one last pat and went inside the house.

When she sat down, she remembers Sunny. Where was he? She had a look through her window, and far off in the paddock she could see Sunny and the fox. Sunny was still chasing the fox and they went round and round the big hollow tree trunk that was lying on the ground. She didn't quite know which one was chasing the other, as they both ran in circles around the tree trunk.

Then suddenly the fox took a sharp turn and disappeared into the forest. Sunny tried his best to follow, but he was getting so huffed and puffed that he had to stop and after one last sniff where the fox had disappeared, he came trotting home. The old woman gave him a pat, and thanked him for chasing the fox away by giving him his favorite treat, a piece of cheese. Then they both went to have a look at the white chicken in the shed. She was much better, so they took her back to the chook house to be with her friends. When the farmer came home from the fields, he went to fix the fence so the chooks were safe for the night.

In the evening the old woman went, in the dark with her torch, to have one last look at her chickens. Not a sound. They were all fast asleep on their perch.

The old woman sighed and looked up at the night sky. It looked like the moon was smiling down at her. When the old woman went to bed, Sunny was already asleep in his bed. The old woman smiled down at him and said, "Thank you Sunny. Goodnight."

# The Old Woman

Once upon a time there was an old woman. She was poor and lived a very simple life. Her knees were aching and she could hardly see, as her eyes were getting old. There were two things that she loved more than anything in the world. One was her dog, Sunny, who was the best retriever in the whole village, and the other was the birds that visited her house. She could listen endlessly to their singing.

Every morning, after her breakfast, which was a piece of bread and some warm milk, she would cut a thin slice of bread and take it outside, where she would put it on a plate. Then she would sit in the sun on her little stool, and wait.

She didn't have to wait for long before her first friend flew down. It was Mr. Yellow Tail. He always sat in the same place at the edge of the plate, so that he could watch the old woman. After a few nibbles, Mr. Yellow Tail would hop onto her knee and start his morning song. Oh, how happy that made the old woman. She would close her eyes and just listen.

While Mr. Yellow Tail was singing, his friends would come to have nibble at the bread. First there were three, then five, and then ten parrots. After they all had a little to eat, they would start to sing their happy songs.

On this morning, when they stopped their singing, they saw how sore and swollen the old woman's knees were. Mr. Yellow Tail called to the other birds, and they all took flight. They flew to the paddock where the sheep were. Mr. Yellow Tail went up to mother sheep and asked if they could get some wool from her. "I have so much wool and I have become slow and heavy. Take as much as you like." The birds took some wool into their beaks, and when Mr. Yellow Tail called to them again, all the birds took flight and followed him.

He flew to the fence where the spiders were weaving their silken webs. Mr. Yellow Tail went to one of the spiders, who was his friend, and asked if he could help the birds make the wool into a blanket."Certainly I will help you," she replied, and she called all the spiders together to help weave the wool into a blanket.

In no time the blanket was ready. Oh, how soft and warm it was. But it was too heavy for the birds to carry by themselves, so Mr. Yellow Tail flew to the old woman's cottage where Sunny, the farm dog, was sitting outside on the front step. He circled above, calling him and Sunny understood that he has to follow the bird.

They came to the fence where the blanket was waiting. Carefully the birds took the blanket down and gave it to Sunny. Sunny, being the best retriever in the whole village, took the blanket to the old woman, who was still sitting in the sun on her little stool. "Where did this come from, Sunny?" She asked the dog. Well, Sunny couldn't say a word, so he just sat there proudly and wagged his tail. The old woman covered her legs with the blanket. It felt so warm and comforting on her sore and swollen knees.

Suddenly, there was the sound of flapping wings; all the birds were coming back. They all landed on and around the bird plate, and all together they started to sing. It was the most beautiful sound the old woman had ever heard."Thank you for the wonderful blanket, Sunny," said the happy old woman, "and thank you birds, for that lovely concert."

To this day the old woman still doesn't know where the blanket came from, for that is a secret between you and I.

# The White Swans

Once upon a time, far away in the north, where the colorful northern lights filled the night sky during the cold winter months, and the lakes were frozen and the trees had their white dresses on, there stood a little log cabin.

Every year when the sun came to this part of the world, the snow started to melt away, the frozen lakes went back to being filled with water, and the birds started to look for places to build their nests in order to have their babies.

It was at this time of the year when after a long, long flight, the white swans would arrive. The winter was too cold for them and they had to fly to warmer countries, but now it was spring again and it was time for them to return. They had to stop in a field to catch their breaths and rest their wings before they could look for a lake where they would build their nests.

This field happened to be right next to the little log cabin, where an old woman lived. The old woman had been waiting for the swans to return. Every day she would look at the sky, through her window, to see the arrival of the birds.

When they landed on the field she saw that the leader of the swans could not walk very well, so the old woman came out and quietly went closer to the bird to find out what was wrong. When she was close enough, she discovered that the swan's leg had a piece of net wrapped around it, and it was very swollen, and bleeding.

"Oh, you poor thing! This must hurt a lot. The pain must have made your journey very difficult."

The swan knew the old woman, as she always gave them food when they arrived, so she let the old woman come closer to see what could be done about her sore leg. The old woman carefully took the piece of net away and covered the leg with green leaves. Then she said, "Maybe you could stay at the lake near my cabin and I can help you to get better." The swan was looking at her very carefully, almost like she knew what the old woman was saying.

The days went by, and the swans found the lake near the old woman's cabin and went to live there. But their leader stayed in the field next to the cabin. Even though the old woman kept a close eye on her,the pain in the swan's leg was still too strong for her to move and build her nest.

Then the woman had a thought. She went to her shed, took out her wheelbarrow, and pushed it into the field. Then she carefully lifted the swan into it and slowly wheeled her down to the grass at the edge of the lake. She carefully lifted the swan out, and then the old woman went and stood on the jetty to watch. After a little while, the bird started to wash the dust off herself and soon the water was splashing everywhere. Then she went into the lake and began to swim with her head held high. The leg was healed.

The old woman stood watching all this and soon another swan came and was keeping her company. Pretty soon the two of them went to start building a nest, where the mother swan could lay her eggs. The old woman was watching this and was very happy. She picked up her wheelbarrow and went back to her nice, cozy little log cabin.

Then one day, the old woman heard a lot of noise coming from the lake, and when she went to see what it was about, well what did she see? Mother and father swan had called to the old woman to come and see their five little babies. That made the old woman very happy, and she quickly went inside to get some dry bread for the whole family.

From that day on, the old woman left dry bread on the rocks near the lake every day for the swans so that they could have a little extra food, and so the babies could grow up big and strong for their next long flight in the winter.

# The Little Village

Once upon a time there was a little island where people lived simple but happy lives in a little village.
They took care of their animals; sheep, cows, horses, chickens, and the trees were full of birds.

One sunny day when one of the mothers was doing some washing near the water, she saw a strange looking cloud over the sea coming towards the island. She left her washing and started to run towards the village, calling "A storm is coming! Find shelter."

People stopped working and rushed inside their houses. The houses were built with heavy logs and they were strong enough to withstand the storm.

When the storm hit the island it blew trees over onto barns and stables, but luckily the animals were in the big meadows and were safe from harm. The boats were smashed by the strong winds, and the people were frightened and the children were crying. It was only a few moments before everything on the island had changed.

Gratually the storm went away and the winds calmed. Slowly the people came out from their houses. They saw how the trees had fallen just outside their front doors. Some couldn't even come out of their houses until the trunks were cleared. All the village people were gathered together and were starting to work out how to help each other, when they heard a voice calling.

"Please! Come and help! My foot is stuck under the tree."

It was Farmer John, who always helped others, and now they were able to help him.

All the strong men got together to move the tree trunk. Then the village doctor came to look at his leg and he put a big bandage around it. There were many other people who needed help too.

Then little Mary said, "My house can become a hospital as my mother has lots of bandages and lots of beds." Mary's mother nodded her head, and said, "Mary is right. Come to our house if you need help."

So all the people who needed help came to Mary's house, where they were given warm drinks and blankets, and Mary and the doctor took care of them all. Afterwards the doctor went to Mary and said, "One day you could be a doctor like me and we could help people together." Mary smiled.

It took a long time to clear all the trees and fix everything that was broken in the storm. The boats, the stables, the barns and a few roofs all needed to be fixed, but soon everything was back to normal and now life is happy again on the little island. More trees have grown and the birds have already made new nests.

# Boy and the Donkey

Once upon a time, there was a donkey, who was well looked after by the people in the village. Every morning he went to visit each house, as he wanted to offer his help to the people. He carried heavy loads of hay and sacks of wheat for farmers and he gave the children rides as well. His fur was soft and shiny and the children loved to pat him.

He knew that people would give him some food in exchange for his help. He loved the dry bread, potatoes, and apples, but his favorites were the carrots. He always left the house where they gave him the carrots until last.

He was not a young donkey anymore and one day he realized that he could not see very well; he couldn't even see where he was going. He tried to use the fences and trees to guide him, walking along beside them, but he still could not find his way to the houses.

After a while he had to stop his morning walks and stay on his own in his little paddock, as he could not see his way around anymore. Where could he get water to drink and who would give him food? Who would pat him and ride on his back? He didn't know what to do.

His thirst had become so great, and he thought, "I have to leave my paddock and try to find some water." So he started to walk towards the trees, using the smells blowing to him on the wind, to guide him. They were the familiar pine trees that he knew very well, and he thought of the squirrels jumping from branch to branch, never falling as they collected pinecones to store in their secret holes.

Now he knew where he was, and he knew that there was a brook nearby where he had drunk from many times before. Oh, how he loved the sound of the running water as it washed over the rocks, making them smooth and round. The donkey followed the sound and came to the brook. He bent his head down to have a long drink. The water tasted delicious on his rough tongue.

Suddenly he heard a voice, "Hello. What is your name? You have very nice ears." The donkey couldn't see the little boy, who was sitting on the rock. The boy kept talking and he told the donkey how he had gotten lost in the big forest.

As they both drank the crystal clear water, the sun started to set behind the hills. Then it got dark very quickly and neither of them could find their way back to the village. Then the donkey lay down to rest, as he was so very tired. The boy lay down too, right next to the donkey. The donkey felt so soft and warm. Soon they both fell asleep.

Early next morning, they were woken up by the song of the rooster. The boy knew who the rooster belonged to in the village, so holding onto the donkey's fur, the boy led him towards the rooster.

Soon they came to the farm gate. That was where the rooster lived. The rooster belonged to the boy's grandfather. Grandfather saw his grandson and the donkey coming. He started to walk towards them. When he was close he embraced his grandson, and then he looked at the donkey, and he could see that his eyes didn't look right.

Grandfather knew what to do. He asked his grandson to get the little brown bottle from his medicine cupboard. Then he put few drops into donkey's eyes. After a while the donkey's eyes started to clear and he was looking around trying to figure out where he was. His ears started to move backwards and forwards. Then the donkey made a loud "Ee-ooh", to thank the grandfather and the boy.The boy looked at his grandfather with a smile.

Now the donkey was able to find his way back to his own paddock and the boy was safe with his grandfather.

# Mary the Little Girl

One evening, after a busy day, mum sat down next to Mary's bed. Mary was lying in bed, looking very worried. So mum asked if something was bothering her.

Mary was quiet for a while, and then she started to tell mum about a boy in her class who keeps hitting and kicking the other children when they are playing. Mary said that she is afraid that one day she might be hit or kicked by this boy.

"Mum, why is he hurting others?" Mary asked.

Mum thought for a while, and then she said, "There might be mornings when some children come to school and they have not had anything to eat or drink, or they are not well and feel uncomfortable being at school. It could be that mum or dad is away and they are missing him or her. Maybe tomorrow I will ask his mother if he would like to visit us this weekend."

"What about if he hurts me when he comes?" Mary asked."I don't think he will," said mum, "I will be there with you and maybe we can bake together." "That would be fun," Mary said.

The next day, when Mary went to school, the boy was not there and he was not there the next day either. He was sick at home, so Mary decided to make a card for him to cheer him up a bit and as the boy lived nearby, she dropped the card in their letterbox on her way home.

The next day the boy was still away. Mary was disappointed, as she would have liked to see how he was.

The next day came and he was not at school.

Then the teacher told the whole class that their friend Peter, had been taken to the hospital. He had a very sore tummy and he needed to stay in the hospital for a few more days. "If someone would like to make him a card, I will be visiting him tomorrow and can take your cards to him," she told them.

Most of the children started to draw pictures for the boy. One drew a flower, another a house, and someone drew a boat.

It took few more days before Peter was able to come back to school and when he arrived with his mum, they had a big cake that Peter and mum had baked for the whole class, as thanks for the cards. Peter's eyes where shining and he looked very happy.

Mary was happy too, as now she didn't have to be afraid to go to school anymore.

# The Earthworm

Once upon a time, not so long ago, there lived a little earthworm in a tiny hole in the soft soil. He happily burrowed his way through the dirt with all his friends, and the soil was healthy and good.

The soil said to himself, "I must remember to thank the worms for their hard work. Without them I would be so hard that nothing would grow on me and I wouldn't look beautiful without flowers and other plants covering me."

But one day the worms could not move. They tried to move, all of them together, but the soil was so hard that they couldn't move an inch. "What's the matter?" called the soil. "I am getting so hard that no plants can grow on me anymore."

"There is no water," replied the worms, "and it is getting dryer and dryer and we cannot move! Oh! It is hard to breathe! There are some strange things on top of us, like paper and tins and plastic.""Now, something has to be done before it is too late!" said the wise little earthworm. "I am going to find out what we can do to fix this." So with all his might the wise little worm wriggled his way out to the farm, and there he saw how the farmer had saved up all his scraps, and his cows' manure and straw to be piled into one big heap. The wise little worm decided to have a taste.

"What a delicious pile this is!" He thought. "I have to show it to the others. There is a lot of work to do." So he wriggled his way back to his friends and told them what he had seen. The others could not wait to go to the farm. It was hard work to get there, but they finally made it.

The work started straight away. Oh, how happy the worms were! They wriggled here and there, and gradually the pile started to change color and release a lovely smell.

One day the farmer went to have a look at how the compost pile was doing. He smiled, and he gave it some water. Then he went to get his tractor, and he filled the trailer with the new, fresh soil that the compost pile had become. Then he drove the tractor to the dry land and emptied the load on top of it. His pockets were full of seeds and with the help of the wind he planted the seeds on the field.

Sister rain saw the new seeds and gave them a generous drink.

Now the field is full of lettuce, carrots, beetroot and potatoes.
"Thank you farmer," said mother Earth.
"Thank you farmer," said the worms.
The life was happy again and everyone had plenty to eat.

# Story of the Hands

Once upon a time, there was a little boy, who lived at the edge of the woods. Every night when the sun went behind the hills, his mother would come and sit next to his bed. They would talk about the day and what they had done.

Mother said that her hands were busy today as she was making muffins for grandmother, who is coming to visit tomorrow. Then she wrote a thank you card to uncle Tom, who came to fix the fences so that the fox cannot get the chickens.

"Oh, I remember Uncle Tom's hands. How big they are" said the boy. "Do all farmers have big hands?" he asked.

"I think most of them do, as they use their hands every day to get the farm work done. But do you remember little Lilly when she was born, how tiny her hands were and how fat her fingers were and how she loved to suck her thumb?"

"Yes, I do remember" said the boy. "And when grandmother put her hand next to little Lilly's hand, it looked so big and wrinkly, and her fingers were bent and the veins looked so knotty. I like looking at peoples' hands. I know a boy, who often keeps his hands in fists. I get a bit worried about him. It sometimes looks like he might hit someone with his fists. I don't like that.

"Are hands made for hitting?" asked the little boy. "No, they are not; they are made to do good things in the world. Your hands can be hard working hands like Uncle Tom's hands or they can be caring and kind hands like grandmother's hands."

"Mother, what kind of hands do I have?" "Well, I hope your hands are kind and helping hands, as those kind of hands will make you happy too."But look, the sun has gone behind the hills and the moon is up with all the bright stars. Now let's look at your hands and see how you cross your fingers, to give thanks for the day and hope that tomorrow will bring more work for our busy hands.

"Goodnight my son."

Printed in the United States
by Baker & Taylor Publisher Services